Tons of Trucks!

TOW TRUCKS

By Martin Harasymiw

Gareth Stevens
PUBLISHING

Please visit our website, www.garethstevens.com. For a free color catalog of all our high-quality books, call toll free 1-800-542-2595 or fax 1-877-542-2596.

Library of Congress Cataloging-in-Publication Data
Names: Harasymiw, Martin, 1978- author.
Title: Tow trucks / Martin Harasymiw.
Description: New York : Gareth Stevens Publishing, [2022] | Series: Tons of trucks! | Includes index. | Audience: Grades K-1
Identifiers: LCCN 2020025923 (print) | LCCN 2020025924 (ebook) | ISBN 9781538262917 (library binding) | ISBN 9781538262894 (paperback) | ISBN 9781538262900 (set) | ISBN 9781538262924 (ebook)
Subjects: LCSH: Wreckers (Vehicles)–Juvenile literature.
Classification: LCC TL230.15 .H368 2022 (print) | LCC TL230.15 (ebook) | DDC 629.225–dc23
LC record available at https://lccn.loc.gov/2020025923
LC ebook record available at https://lccn.loc.gov/2020025924

First Edition

Published in 2022 by
Gareth Stevens Publishing
111 East 14th Street, Suite 349
New York, NY 10003

Editor: Therese Shea
Designer: Deanna Paternostro

Photo credits: Cover Ronald Rampsch/Shutterstock.com; p. 5 luis2499/Shutterstock.com; p. 7 kozmoat98/iStock/Getty Images Plus/Getty Images; p. 9 Harshit Srivastava S3/Shutterstock.com; pp. 11, 24 (right) Wollertz/Shutterstock.com; pp. 13, 24 (center) Ulina_C/iStock/Getty Images Plus; p. 15 Andyqwe/iStock/Getty Images Plus; p. 17 F Armstrong Photography/Shutterstock.com; p. 19 leezsnow/E+/Getty Images; p. 21 romul014/Shutterstock.com; p. 23 Helena Wahlman/Maskot/Getty Images; p. 24 (left) Robert Crum/Shutterstock.com.

Printed in the United States of America

CPSIA compliance information: Batch #CSGS22: For further information contact Gareth Stevens, New York, New York at 1-800-542-2595.

Contents

My Favorite Truck 4

Different Kinds 8

How They Help 16

Words to Know 24

Index 24

This is my toy truck.
It's a tow truck!

UNDER
CONSTRUCTION

This is a real tow truck!
It moves cars.

Some trucks
lift two wheels.
Then they pull the car.

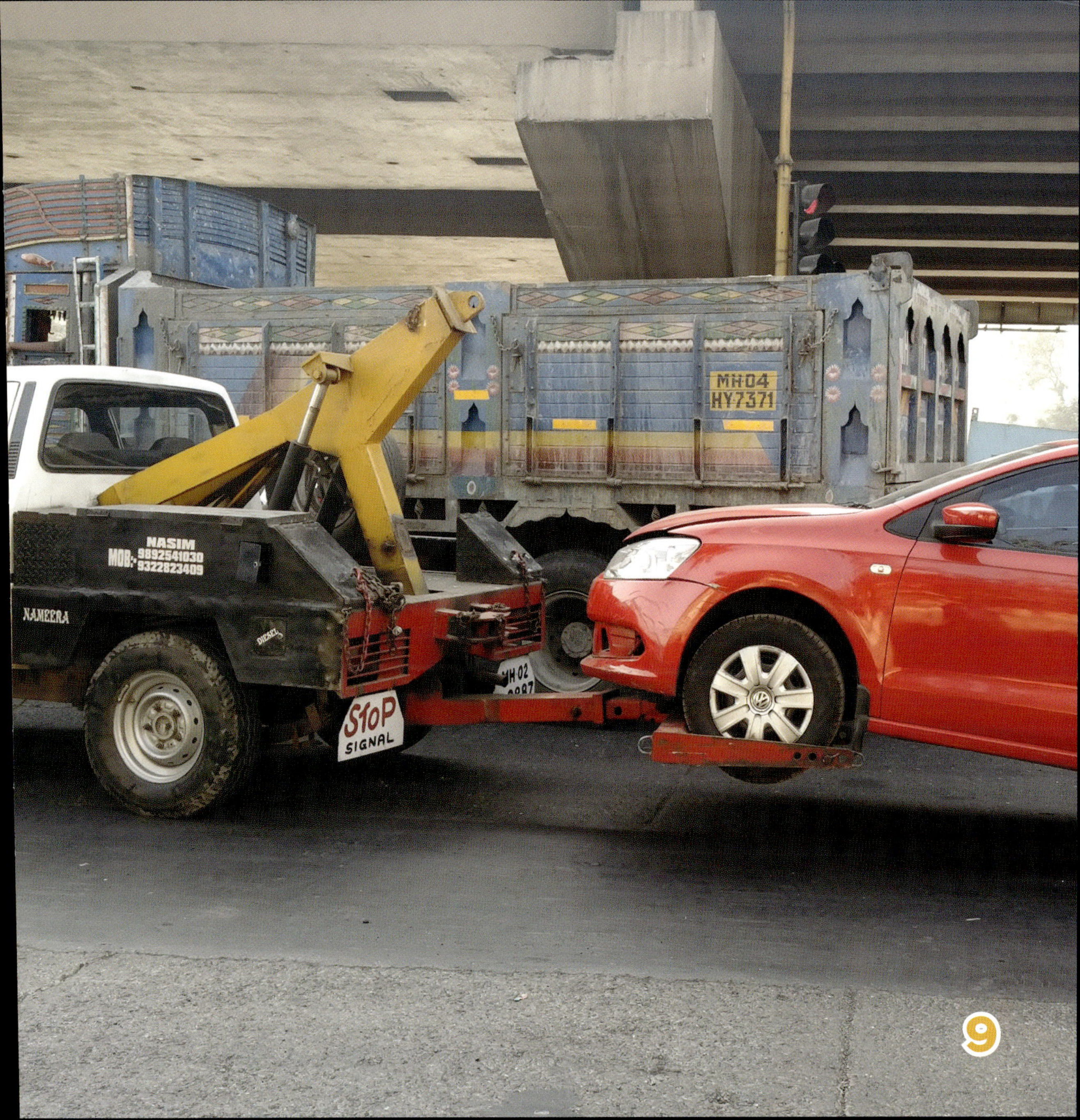
MH04
HY7371
NASIM
MOB:- 9892541030
9322823409
NAMEERA
STOP
SIGNAL

Some trucks
have a flatbed.
It slides down.
Cars move onto it.

RUBICON
Jeep
SERVING BROOKINGS, GOLD BEACH, AND PORT ORFORD

Some trucks
have a boom.
The boom lifts
cars onto the truck!

There are tow trucks
for big trucks!

Tow trucks help cars that break down.

They help cars
in accidents.

They take cars
to be fixed.

Tow trucks help!

Words to Know

accident

boom

flatbed

Index

accident 18
flatbed 10
boom 12
wheels 8